# Before We Said Hello

MUSIC
FOR THE
SOUL

# Before We Said Hello

Finding Hope
after Pregnancy Loss
and Infant Loss

*devotionals by*
BECKY NORDQUIST
with stories by guest contributors

credo
house publishers

ISBN: 978-1-62586-149-8

Cover and interior design by Sharon VanLoozenoord
Editing by Triple M Editorial Services, LLC

*Printed in the United States of America*
First edition

# BEFORE WE SAID HELLO

We were so excited
What anticipation
We'd prepared a place for you inside our hearts
Oh, how you were wanted
We had plans and dreams
Then in an instant it all came apart

Like a flower that was crushed before it could bloom
Like a story just begun that ended much too soon
We grieve love interrupted that has no place to go
We said goodbye before we said hello

They say you're in Heaven
and someday I'll see you
But that doesn't fill the ache I'm feeling now
Your life was so special
Such a miracle
Now life goes on but I just don't know how

Like a flower that was crushed before it could bloom
Like a story just begun that ended much too soon
We grieve the child who's living in our hearts but not our home
We said goodbye before we said hello

You are my angel and we'll never be apart
I may not hold in my arms but I'll still hold you in my heart

Like a flower that was crushed before it could bloom
Like a story just begun that ended much too soon
We grieve the hopes cut short
The memories we'll never know
Why? Tell me why...
Why did we have to say goodbye before we said hello?

From the depths of despair, O LORD,
I call for your help.
Hear my cry, O LORD.
Pay attention to my prayer.

PSALM 130:1-2 NLT

When you least expect it, another trigger sends you spiraling downward. You wonder if life will ever return to the way it was before you were forced to say goodbye.

No parent should outlive his or her child, yet here you are, trying not to feel the pain. You have never before sunk into a hole as deep as this one. The darkness threatens to overtake you and chokes breath from your already exhausted soul.

Barely able to form the name, you whisper again . . . "Jesus . . . help."

We long for Him to remove the inconsolable ache within us. We long for Him to remove the flashes of gore that remind us of the end of our babies. We long for deliverance from the pain. Instead, Jesus comes with His presence. He comes bearing strength. He comes bearing peace that we simply cannot understand. He fills us as we inhale and strengthens us as we exhale. When we think we cannot take one more step or raise our head one more time, He holds us together and we survive.

But you, O LORD, are a shield about me,
my glory, and the lifter of my head. (Psalm 3:3 ESV)

Do you need to cry out in despair? Write out your lament. Jesus hears your prayers and catches your tears. There is nothing wasted when we hand things over to Him . . . nothing. He comes in the most uncommon ways, but He is always faithful to show up.

_____

_____

_____

_____

_____

_____

_____

_____

_____

_____

_____

_____

_____

## DAY 2

As the deer pants for streams of water,
so my soul pants for you, my God.
My soul thirsts for God, for the living God.
When can I go and meet with God?
My tears have been my food day and night,
while people say to me all day long,
"Where is your God?"

PSALM 42:1-3

Many wondered where Dave and I found the strength to stand as we traversed 20 months of continual loss: two miscarriages; the stillbirth of our son Niklas; the losses of my mom, my brother, and my father-in-law; and finding my dear friend dead of a heart attack in our family room.

Trauma and grief can either root us more deeply *in* God or cause us to run away. Deciding we will consistently turn toward Him in trauma and loss *before* it comes is a crucial decision.

This doesn't mean we ignore pain or throw Christianese answers at painful questions. Honest wrestling is crucial to our growth. This is where our relationship with God gets real. Acknowledging that He is always present and holding to the truth of His word are essential. This is true even if we can't feel His presence, see promises coming to fruition yet, or understand what happened.

We cling to God and His word, not our circumstances, not our emotions, and not our control over things. He is our solid rock and foundation when the earthly foundation of our life gives way. We choose to turn inward and ask questions of our Lord in the middle of the heartache and confusion. We choose to search for His hand in the middle of what we cannot understand. When we choose Him, we choose hope.

_____

_____

_____

_____

_____

_____

_____

_____

_____

_____

_____

_____

_____

# HOPE AND A FUTURE
*Kylie Scott*

For my husband and me, November 16, 2017, was the most joyous day of our lives. That day we found out we were pregnant . . . finally. We had struggled for six long years to have our little one. I remember jumping up and down with excitement and crying happy tears. We called our close friends and family because we were not going to wait another moment.

January 5 was the day we went in to hear our baby's heartbeat. By that time, I was eleven weeks along. On the way to the doctor's appointment we were giddy, discussing names and dreams we had for this baby. We had waited so long.

But when we got to the office, we were told our baby had no heartbeat. We went in as the happiest couple in the world and left with our hearts broken. The doctor said I had lost the baby around six weeks, and my body just hadn't released it yet. I'd had a "missed miscarriage." For five whole weeks, I had been a walking tomb and didn't realize it. I went from having a womb to a tomb.

I thought about how cruel it was for my body to allow me to believe I was still carrying a healthy baby. I'd had no symptoms of miscarrying. In fact, I experienced pregnancy symptoms well after I found out I had lost the baby. The doctor was worried I would get sepsis since I had already carried the baby for five weeks by the time we discovered it had been gone. So I went ahead and had the baby removed under anesthesia. We felt betrayed by God. I felt God had blessed us with this gift we had repeatedly asked for, only to take it away. I struggled with this thought.

In the days ahead, I would soon come to know who my true friends were. I lost relationships due to the fact that people did not know how to respond. They just quit talking to us altogether. To this day there are some who have not acknowledged that we lost our baby, and that *hurts*. Most of the support I did get was from people saying things like "You can always have another one," "At least you know you can get pregnant," or even "It was for the best, something was wrong." People need to know those things cut deep. People have good intentions, and I remind myself of that. But churches and communities need to raise awareness about how to respond when someone loses a child.

Although the pain of losing our baby still hurts today, I have grown to lean into God even more. We have not been able to conceive again, so we have chosen to foster babies in honor of our little one. I am reminded daily of Jeremiah 29:11: "For I know the plans I have for you . . . plans to prosper you and not to harm you, plans to give you hope and a future."

Sometimes the process is painful, but I trust Him.

## DAY 3

All my longings lie open before you, Lord;
my sighing is not hidden from you.
My heart pounds, my strength fails me;
even the light has gone from my eyes.
My friends and companions avoid me
because of my wounds;
my neighbors stay far away.

PSALM 38:9-11

In the aftermath of infant loss, the blanket of grief can cover us for what seems like forever. Many people do not understand the deep grief associated with the loss of a pregnancy or a stillborn baby. They deliver "well-meaning" words and trite clichés in hopes of stifling our wounded cries. The litany of "at least" statements they often offer only inflicts fresh and painful wounds.

"At least you have other children." "At least you can have more or try again." "At least you were only x amount of weeks along." At least . . . I always wanted to reply, "At least you aren't the one choosing a casket for your baby, deciding what to dress him in, or whether or not to place toys and your favorite books into the ground with him."

At least.

The people you thought would remain faithfully by your side disappear into the shadows. Many duck and walk the other way to avoid asking you how you are doing. They avoid you because of your wounds, and you look heavenward, enduring more tears of loss you didn't expect.

Our sighing is not hidden from Him. He hears your cries; He sees your wounds. Those who remain alongside you are those you will remember. Those who come to the funeral, sit at your side, call you, come to the birthday celebration of your lost little one . . . they are gifts and true blessings. But even if there is no one, we are never alone. God is always with us.

Write out the hurtful things you've been told. Choose today to forgive those people. Write down their names and write out your forgiveness for what they did and said. If there is someone who has been especially toxic, it's okay to distance yourself for a time to remain safe, but forgive them. Hand them over to the One Who will take care of you . . . and them.

_____

_____

_____

_____

_____

_____

_____

_____

_____

## DAY 4

My soul is in deep anguish.
How long, Lᴏʀᴅ, how long?
Turn, Lᴏʀᴅ, and deliver me;
save me because of your unfailing love. . . .
I am worn out from my groaning.
All night long I flood my bed with weeping
and drench my couch with tears.
My eyes grow weak with sorrow . . .

Psᴀʟᴍ 6:3–7

It is often at night when our grief comes unwanted and with full force. Flashes of memories both excruciating and gruesome exhaust our hearts. We lay in silence missing the one we had to whisper goodbye to before we even had the chance to say hello. No one sees the tears we cry or the silent screams we muffle with our pillows.

Except there *is* One who sees every single tear, who knows our wounded and broken hearts.

Lament is not a failure of faith. Lament is a beautiful gesture of crying out in honest pain to our gracious, loving God. He sees and understands situations and sorrows we cannot comprehend. Asking Him to bring comfort and calm into chaotic places is an act of faith. When we cry out, He holds us close and offers Himself as a refuge on this dark journey we seemingly tread alone.

Please use the space provided to journal your honest lament, and ask the hard questions. There isn't anything God doesn't know about your struggle, pain, or journey. Do not fear being open and truthful with Him. He loves you more than you can imagine. He loves enough for you to trust Him with your confusion, your agony, and your rage. He is a big God. He can handle big questions, big pain, and big emotions.

_____

_____

_____

_____

_____

_____

_____

_____

_____

_____

_____

_____

_____

_____

_____

_____

_____

_____

_____

# DAY 5

Why, LORD, do you stand far off?
Why do you hide yourself in times of trouble?

PSALM 10:1

How long, LORD? Will you forget me forever?
How long will you hide your face from me?
How long must I wrestle with my thoughts
and day after day have sorrow in my heart? . . .
But I trust in your unfailing love;
my heart rejoices in your salvation.
I will sing the LORD's praise,
for he has been good to me.

PSALM 13:1-2, 5-6

Silence.

Silence shattered the room when you were told the baby you'd anticipated was not arriving. Your plans and dreams for that precious little life?

Silenced.

There would be no tiny pink toes. No first cry. Instead, silence. Silence as your heart cried out to God, "Why?!"

There are times when God feels distant, even nonexistent in your trauma, as though He disappeared with the death of your child into silence and emptiness.

You wonder if He has forgotten you. "How long will my sorrow last? How long will it feel as though I cannot lift my head from the pillow? How long before I stop rushing to the bathroom to silently sob when I see a pregnancy announcement or hear a newborn baby cry? How long, Lord, will my sorrow last?"

His answer does not come in the form of rescue *from* this journey. Rather, He becomes a refuge as you walk *through* it. As you cry for mercy and relief from the grief, He meets you with His quiet presence, sometimes so subtle and so still that you can miss Him.

He hears your silent screams. He has been beside you the whole time and will walk every step of this grueling journey with you. Like a whisper, His Truth resides within you. He holds you, even though you can't always feel it. The fact that you open your eyes to greet another day is evidence He has never left you.

"I will never leave you nor forsake you." (Hebrews 13:5 ESV)

Write out your fear, your hurt, and your thoughts in the silence. How has silence spoken to you? Write out the truth about His presence even when you don't feel it. Look for ways throughout the day that you see His presence, and write them down.

_____

_____

_____

_____

_____

_____

_____

# I WILL SAY HELLO

*Iris Delesantro*

I would have celebrated my daughter Jessica Jean's 36th birthday this year. But I never got to celebrate any birthdays with her. I had to say goodbye to her before I got a chance to say hello. Jessica was stillborn, and 36 years later, memories of her still bring tears as I write. Her two brothers would have been great with her.

Losing her hurt us all so much. I had just been through a miscarriage the year before, but the pain of losing Jessica broke my heart. I learned what it meant and felt like to have your heart broken. I really didn't allow myself to grieve as I should have. Once after crying, I was told by someone very close to me to "just bury it and let it go already." It had only been a few weeks since we had lost Jessica. I was mad at God for taking her. Her death destroyed my marriage, and I buried the pain within and didn't speak of it.

........................................................................

My depression became worse. Tears always came on her birthday and Christmas Eve when I heard "Silent Night" (it never failed).

But God's grace has pulled me through. As I came to know Him, He alone was able to heal my broken heart. I now know that my babies are in heaven, and one day I will say hello to them.

I pray for anyone who has been through this kind of loss that they get close to God and allow Him to heal them as they go through their grieving. I pray God would strengthen them and overwhelm them with His peace like only He can give.

In Our Lord's mighty name.

Blessings!

...............................                           ...............................

DAY 6

My heart is in anguish within me;
the terrors of death have fallen on me.
Fear and trembling have beset me;
horror has overwhelmed me.
I said, "Oh that I had the wings of a dove!
I would fly away and be at rest.
I would flee far away
and stay in the desert;
I would hurry to my place of shelter,
far from the tempest and storm."

PSALM 55:4-8

Waves of anguish crash over you, threatening to drag you under. Days come where you wish you could run away and escape the sorrow that consumes each breath. Perhaps a time travel machine would help and take you back to life before your innocence was ripped from you. Your life has come to a screeching halt, and you watch as the world continues to rapidly spin.

"Don't they know what's happened? Don't they understand life has stopped?" you cry out.

The world goes on as if your baby never existed. You're stuck, and everyone else speeds forward. You're torn apart, never to be the same again, and everyone else moves on. You sit silently on the sidelines of life watching the rushing and meaningless banter. It seems everyone has forgotten the life you held so close and cherished, as if your baby's life never happened.

You ask yourself, "Will I ever re-enter the game? Will I ever return to normal? Will life ever be the same?"

The answer is yes . . . and no.

Yes, you will learn to move forward. Will you be the same? No. You've been thrust into a front-row seat to witness the fragility of life. Therefore, you cannot walk life's path in the same way you once did. You've been forced to join an exclusive club of parents who have lost a child. It's a club none of us want to be a member of. Yet here we are.

We want to run from this painful place. We dash everywhere trying to find relief. We thrust ourselves into busyness: hobbies, friends, cleaning, work, travel, food, alcohol, shopping, or drugs. We race around hoping to find rest and refuge from the pain. But nothing and no one can replace the empty space left behind by our babies. Only the eternal God can fill the void within us. Only He can be our peace and rest.

He sits with you in that emptiness. He holds you in the loss and teaches you how to move forward. He fills you with the strength and ability to come alongside others to comfort them in their grief. He is faithful. He loves you. He cries with you. Run to your resting place . . . His arms. You will find that God alone can satisfy the longings of your wounded heart.

Where would you like to run to if you could? Where are you tempted to run in search of rest and peace other than God? What does walking forward with your loss look like, if you can imagine it?

_____

_____

_____

_____

I waited patiently for the LORD;
he turned to me and heard my cry.
He lifted me out of the slimy pit,
out of the mud and mire;
he set my feet on a rock
and gave me a firm place to stand.
He put a new song in my mouth,
a hymn of praise to our God.
Many will see and fear the LORD
and put their trust in him.

PSALM 40

Patience.

Most of us struggle with it, especially during suffering. We want answers. We want relief, and we want it now. We cry out, "How long will I feel this way? How long will my heart be sick?" We wonder if we will ever feel normal again.

Deep down, we realize that we will never be the same. It isn't possible to be the person we were before the earthly life of our child was cut short. It feels like the love meant for this child has no place to go.

The pit is deep. It grows dark and cold. Few understand it . . . yet there is One who lovingly reaches down to lift us out.

Some days, He crawls down into the pit and silently sits with us in the ache. We yearn for a voice to sing again. He is good and graciously restores what has been broken and seemingly lost. Though the song will sound different than before tragedy entered our lives, it will be glorious as we hand over the melody and lyrics to Him. He is faithful to us in every moment of our suffering when we give our pain completely to Him.

Write out your dreams and desires. How would you love to see God use your journey for something good? Can you already see how He is using your life, your baby's life, to help others in their ache? How? How is He restoring your voice? What "lyric" of your life song do you hope will come from this experience?

_____

_____

_____

_____

_____

_____

_____

_____

_____

_____

_____

_____

_____

# CHOOSING TRUST

*Christy Wood*

$A$s I lay looking at the ultrasound monitor, I didn't need anyone to tell me. I knew as soon as I saw him. My baby was dead.

Not long after, we sat silently waiting for the doctor in a small room filled with multiple Kleenex boxes. Four weeks ago, our baby was wiggling all over that monitor waving to us, measuring just right. And now he was dead. Why would God do this to us again?

We had just lost our first baby seven months ago. By the time I started miscarrying at eighteen weeks, he was already absorbing into my uterus, so I had to have a D&C. It was the hardest thing I'd ever gone through.

We had been far more careful this time. There had been many more ultrasounds, and things had been looking good. It seemed like God was answering our prayers, but now my heart was breaking all over again. Why would God let this happen?

The doctor finally came. He said that our baby was bigger this time and told me it would be better if I delivered him. He wanted to know if tomorrow—Valentine's Day—would work.

Valentine's Day will never be the same for me. I spent February 14, 2009, in the hospital laboring with my tiny baby. It was surreal. To be on the maternity floor. To hear other babies crying. Labor lasted all day until finally, at 9:34 p.m., we got to see our teeny little baby boy. He was about fifteen weeks along with tiny fingers and toes and little ribs. You could even see his fingernails starting to form. The nurses let us spend as much time as we wanted with him. When I hear the phrase "heart-wrenching grief," I know exactly what it means. Holding my son, it felt like my chest was ripping into two. I wanted that baby so much! But I wanted him to be alive. And he wasn't.

A nurse came and asked if we had a name for him. I didn't have any names for dead babies, only for living ones. We didn't know what to do. My husband and I were struggling to trust God and believe in His goodness. It felt impossible. So we chose to take a crazy step of faith, and we named our son Trust. Not because we felt it, but because we didn't. We chose to trust in a God that we could not see and did not understand. And instantly, I felt a strange peace flood my soul.

I know what it means in Philippians 4:7: "And the peace of God, which transcends all understanding, will guard your hearts and your minds in Christ Jesus." I know what it means because the peace I felt didn't make any sense. Nothing had changed in my circumstances, and I still grieved deeply, but I also had absolute peace. Although I still didn't understand God, I discovered His goodness and love in the middle of my pain.

## DAY 8

Hear my prayer, LORD,
listen to my cry for help;
do not be deaf to my weeping.

PSALM 39:12

At times, it can feel as though your prayers hit the ceiling, only to fall unanswered back into your soul. Our words seem to fall on deaf ears, yet we know God is not deaf.

We want the suffering to stop. We beg Him for relief from pain, and it cannot come quickly enough. It appears God either doesn't hear or doesn't care.

But neither one of these assumptions is the truth: God not only hears but He cares more than you could imagine.

Trust that He will meet you in your sorrow. Trust that He is working out something incredible, something eternal, something that will bring blessing for you and glory for the kingdom of God.

Your prayers do not fall on deaf ears; they fall into the loving heart of your Father in heaven. Your Father, who will never leave you or forsake you. Your Father, who weeps with you. Your Father, who loves you and your baby more than you could ever imagine.

How are you suffering? Write an honest prayer to your heavenly Father.

_____

_____

_____

_____

_____

_____

_____

_____

_____

_____

_____

_____

_____

# DAY 9

Be merciful to me, LORD,
for I am in distress:
my eyes grow weak with sorrow,
my soul and my body with grief.
My life is consumed by anguish
and my years by groaning;
my strength fails
because of my affliction,
and my bones grow weak.

PSALM 31:9-10

The morning sun seemingly mocks the grief that consumes your heart. You barely possess the strength to walk through another day. You awake relying on the Creator to lift your head because another breath is barely possible in your own strength. Simply walking through a grocery store makes you physically ache. You want to groan, but you push through.

The loss of a baby is not something we "get over." Instead, with halting, agonizing steps, we learn to move forward. We hold hands with grief and embrace each moment, knowing not to take anything for granted. We learn to honor our babies who remain unseen to this world because their lives matter to us and to God.

It doesn't matter how many weeks, months, days, or hours your child was alive. Whether that life was lived inside or outside the womb, your child's life was precious and *priceless*. Your sorrow is valid. Your grief is important.

God sees our daily ache and is merciful. He hears the cries of our hearts. He sees the anguish that can overtake us, and

He walks with us, whispering His love in a multitude of ways. We just need to ask for eyes to see and ears to hear. Though often we do not feel it, His strength carries us through yet another unbearable day. He grows virtues and strengths in us that we could not have imagined.

Write about how your body responds to the ache in your heart. How do you best sense His love for you? Are you struggling to believe that He loves you? What are the things that are helping you focus on moving forward?

_____

_____

_____

_____

_____

_____

_____

_____

_____

_____

_____

_____

# BROKEN SEEDS

*Andrew Hamlet*

..................................................................................

The tears poured down my face, forced out by a hurt I hadn't known was there. I tried helplessly to stop them.

It was December 2017, a couple days after Christmas. My wife had taken a trip to California to visit her childhood best friend. We thought it would lift her spirits. I sat alone at home trying to figure out why this grown man was overcome with such grief that it brought him to his knees.

My wife and I had just suffered our third miscarriage in a year and half. Even though we already had three boys and a girl, we had opened our hearts to have one more child. Having babies had never been a problem before. Stop *not* trying and boom—a month later, a baby was on the way. This time, instead of making a baby, we conceived pain and hurt on a level I didn't know existed. We conceived doubt, fear, and questions that kept us up at night.

The first time, I was a good husband. I held my wife. I even cried a little with her, but I felt distant—like it was all happening to her. The baby was in *her* body. The bond was between *her* and that baby. I didn't even get to hold him or her.

..................................................................................

The second miscarriage was when doubt and questions set in. *Is this worth all the pain? What if we're doing something God doesn't want, and He's trying to tell us?*

I hadn't realized it until that day on my knees that a tsunami of guilt, shame, and pain had built up in my heart. I'd dammed it up with work and video games; dulled it with lifting weights and playing sports. Grief will not be outrun; it cannot be escaped. It will catch you off guard and all at once.

*Why, God? How could you? What were we doing wrong?* My tears came faster than I could wipe them. First I felt shame. As a man, I wanted to stop it, use my strength and heal what was broken, but I was powerless. I felt weak. I would have given my life for any three of my lost children to live. Then, in that mess, while I was drowning in grief, I felt God's arms around me. I didn't need answers to my questions. There were no answers. I needed God to give me permission to acknowledge what I had lost. I stopped fighting the tears and let them flow.

## DAY 10

Hear my cry, O God;
listen to my prayer.
From the ends of the earth
I call to you,
I call as my heart grows faint;
lead me to the rock that
is higher than I.

PSALM 61:1-2

Have you ever felt like your grief has sent you to the ends of the earth? That you've been exiled into dark, unfamiliar territory? Banished from a life you once possessed, an innocence you once knew, and left to wander in uncharted lands? The journey can be exhausting and cause your heart to falter.

In these moments, as we mourn the loss of our sweet children, we can cry out in honesty to a God who is always with us. He is faithful to lead us to a rock of refuge that is higher than we are, safer than our emotions, and more secure than our weakened hearts. . . Himself.

As we press into Him as our safe haven, relinquishing things we cannot understand, He reveals Who He is and offers us a taste of His all-sufficient grace and unending love for us. He lifts us above the dark clouds and gives us perspective and hope we cannot find any other way. He shares our tears, calms our fears, and makes a way to see a new path forward . . . visible only when we stand on the Lord as our Rock.

Write out the cry of your heart today. Perhaps it isn't a cry of lament, but a faint song of hope coming through the pain. Pour out your heart to Him, resting assured that as you seek Him, He will guide you to Himself, our Rock of security.

_____

_____

_____

_____

_____

_____

_____

_____

_____

_____

_____

_____

_____

_____

# DAY 11

Save me, O God,
for the waters have come up to my neck.
I sink in the miry depths,
where there is no foothold.
I have come into the deep waters;
the floods engulf me.
I am worn out calling for help;
my throat is parched.
My eyes fail, looking for my God.

PSALM 69:1–3

Many of us have suffered multiple losses. Dave and I had 5 pregnancy losses and one stillbirth in just over two years. There were times when it seemed as though we couldn't get our heads above the waters of sorrow. The solidity of our lives dissipated into nothingness, our dreams and hopes abruptly cut short.

Submerged in the shadows of despair, we can often grow weary. We search for God, but trying to gain understanding and asking the questions of "why" and "what if" can overwhelm and exhaust us.

In honest conversation and questions, we find God. Caring for your mind, body, and spirit is critical. If one is out of balance, the other areas suffer. Seeking support through safe people, a therapist, or a support group can be helpful. Isolation can be dangerous.

The enemy loves to cut us off from others. When he gets us alone, he whispers lies that cause doubt and depression to set in. His number one objective is to steal, kill, and destroy. He seeks this for all members of the human race. His hatred toward God extends to hatred for anyone created in God's image. Your baby, your family, and you are all his targets. His greatest achievement would be to separate you from God. The enemy's ultimate goal is to get you to believe that God doesn't understand, isn't good, and doesn't care. He wants to destroy you, incapacitate you, and render you useless.

Often, we don't feel like throwing on praise music or going for an invigorating walk in God's creation. We need to make the choice that today, or even for the next five minutes, we will reach out and reach up! Remaining in His care means taking care of yourself. Feed your soul with the rich feast of His word, your mind by putting only good things into it, and your body by getting proper nutrition and enough rest. In so doing, you will begin to heal your heart.

What are some steps you need to take in the area of self-care?

_____

_____

_____

_____

_____

_____

_____

_____

_____

Have mercy on me, my God,
have mercy on me,
for in you I take refuge.
I will take refuge in the shadow
of your wings
until the disaster has passed.
I cry out to God Most High,
to God, who vindicates me.

PSALM 57:1-2

"How could this be your purpose for me? How could this bring hope and a future? Certainly, a God who cares wouldn't do this!"

I pleaded with the mocking blue sky trimmed with puffy white clouds. I'd followed faithfully, or so I thought. So, why would God allow *this* to happen?

I lay in the spring sunshine and paused for an answer. I lingered for a moment at the thought of His love and care . . . did it really apply to me? Was *this* proof that it didn't? I wrestled with my faith in a way I'd never had the guts to do before. I asked my questions, praying for answers and looking in His word as I listened for His still, small voice to speak truth to my frail, wounded heart.

Suddenly, my honest questioning broke through a barrier between us. My relationship with Him grew deeper the more questions I asked and the more I sought Him. I read through stories from ages past, seeing the broken, fallen world for what it is.

God's purpose always has eternal benefit. His purpose is always about restoring us to Himself. His purpose is always for our good and His glory. He wastes not one step of your journey or mine. He will use whatever we lay before His throne, and He will do amazing things through it.

What question are you most afraid to ask God? Why? Take that question and write it out. Pray over it. Open God's word and seek the answer. If you have trouble, seek out your pastor or a trusted friend who is familiar with the word of God. Most of all, relinquish the one question we all want to ask most . . . *Why me?* Understand there are questions we will not get answers to this side of heaven. Choose to be okay with an unanswered question. This comes down to an issue of trust. Childlike trust. Trust that He will reveal to you what you need to know when you need to know it . . . or *if* you need to know it.

_____

_____

_____

_____

_____

_____

_____

_____

_____

_____

# EVERY SINGLE CHILD

*Julie Reuschel*

...............................................................................

Our story is a story of grief, trust, miracles, and hope.

In 2016, at our 20-week ultrasound, the doctors told us that our daughter was very sick. They informed us that she would probably pass away fairly soon, in the coming weeks. We immediately began begging God to heal our daughter. Weeks followed and she continued to grow and kick and roll around in my belly. At every appointment, though her heart was strong, the doctors still did not think she was going to make it.

Slowly, our prayers began to change. We knew God had the power to heal, and we prayed every day for that. But we also began asking Him to allow us to meet her. If she was going to pass away from this disorder, could we please meet her and spend some time with her first?

Well, God allowed me to carry her to full term, and at 37 weeks she was born. We labored for 26 hours, not knowing whether she was going have a heartbeat. And 26 hours later, she was born, but without a heartbeat. Our pediatrician later told us that in those first moments, he did the only thing he

...............................................................................

could think to do for our little family, and that was to say a prayer. And at that moment, her heart started beating.

God gave us a miracle that day. No, He did not heal her, but He answered our prayer, our cry to meet her and spend precious time with her. Our miracle was 45 minutes with our little girl, Faith.

The days and months that followed were the hardest we have ever had to live through. We had to plan a funeral and say goodbye much too soon. One day at a time, one hour at a time, sometimes one minute at a time, was the only way we made it through those moments. God got us through those days; He gave us strength when we had nothing left. He carried us when our hearts were too heavy. He brought people into our lives we couldn't have done without. He listened and cried with us. But, best of all, because of His son dying for us, we have the promise of seeing our daughter again one day.

## DAY 13

I cried out to God for help;
I cried out to God to hear me.
When I was in distress, I sought the Lord;
at night I stretched out untiring hands
and I would not be comforted.
I remembered you, God, and I groaned;
I meditated, and my spirit grew faint.
You kept my eyes from closing;
I was too troubled to speak.
I thought about the former days,
the years of long ago;
I remembered my songs in the night.
My heart meditated and my spirit asked:
"Will the Lord reject forever?
Will he never show his favor again?
Has his unfailing love vanished forever?
Has his promise failed for all time?"

PSALM 77:1–8

The quiet of the night grows long as you lie in the stillness. Each moment, you yearn to awake to cries and coos of the little one you so deeply yearned for. Yet you lie in the silence, seeing only a path with no happy ending.

No words come, just an ache. No song, just an unrelenting groan. Death feels a breath away; you know a piece of you died with your baby.

Yet God continues to wake you each morning, and in this you know He has a purpose for you. He wouldn't open your eyes if there wasn't a reason for you to continue to exist on earth.

"What good could possibly come from this?" you ask, you plead through angry tears at times.

You look back and remember times past. Times where you clearly saw God take something difficult, painful, or even impossible and turn it around. He flipped the script. There was suddenly purpose for the pain and a reason to stand in the suffering. His love did not leave. His purpose never failed.

You want desperately to feel that way now. Though the broken world has crushed a dream, you believe that God is determined to waste nothing we go through. Hope comes alive as we hand our sufferings over to Him—either in us or in others through the honest telling of our stories.

Take a moment to recall God's faithfulness in your life. Ask the Holy Spirit to show you where He has loved you, protected you, or taken bad moments and used them for something positive. Write those moments out. Thank God for them. Ask Him to show you His faithfulness in *this* journey. Ask for eyes to see how He will use you and your baby's life for a positive purpose.

_____

_____

_____

_____

_____

_____

_____

_____

Blessed are those whose strength is in you,
Whose hearts are set on pilgrimage.
As they pass through the Valley of Baka,
they make it a place of springs;
the autumn rains also cover it with pools.
They go from strength to strength,
till each appears before God in Zion.

PSALM 84:5-7

A valley. Perhaps the darkest, most barren valley you've ever faced. Where does it lead? Where are you headed in this dry, dark, unknown valley of life?

On the way to the temple, the psalmist would pass through the Valley of Baka. Baka can mean "weeping." The psalmist may have been speaking of struggles and sorrows people must pass through on their way to meet God.

We have a choice about where we set our heart on this journey. We can choose to set our heart on a pilgrimage toward the presence of God in all sorrows, or we can choose to turn away as we walk through the Valley of Baka of our lives. We can choose to see it as barren and without purpose, or we can embrace it and see it for the opportunity it is—to experience more of His presence and person, and to know our God more intimately and personally.

When we do, we will experience a peace that is beyond what we can understand. We will rise from ashes in strength that is not of this world. This is when the barren, dry places of this valley become vibrant springs, full of life.

What is the greatest sorrow in your "Valley of Baka" right now? Write it out. Ask for God to give you eyes to see and ears to hear the ways He is calling you deeper into His presence. Ask Him to be able to clearly see the invitation He is holding out for you. Write out what you see. Remember, as you draw near to Him, He draws near to you.

_____

_____

_____

_____

_____

_____

_____

_____

_____

_____

_____

_____

_____

_____

# DAY 15

> You have taken from me friend and neighbor;
> darkness is my closest friend.
>
> PSALM 88:18

"When are you going to get over this?"

"At least you weren't that far along."

"At least you can have more children."

"At least you have other children."

"Why do you keep reliving this?"

"It just wasn't meant to be."

"This is just God's way of saying this baby wasn't supposed to be here."

"God must have needed another angel."

"I just can't handle you crying like this all the time."

Oh, the things well-meaning people say in our times of grieving! Often we find ourselves needing to distance ourselves from those who think they "know" the answer to the "why" question; who tend to say things that hurt instead of help.

The most healing friend is the one who simply sits in the quiet ache alongside you, saying nothing, just offering to hold you and share your tears. No cliché or platitude is offered, just love and presence. For there *is* no good answer, no words that can erase the pain of what is. Nothing anyone could say or do will take away the sorrow of your world in this moment.

Sometimes we find that people disappear from our lives. Those who we thought would be present and walk with us back away slowly and turn away. People do this for different reasons. Maybe they don't know what to say. Or maybe they're like one woman who, as I shared my story, stopped me, saying, "I just can't listen to this; it's just too painful to hear."

In these isolating moments, the air around us grows dark. It seems no one understands the hell we are living, and sometimes it seems that no one cares.

But God cares. He sits in the darkness with you. You can cry out, complain, and express your deepest sorrow. He will offer no cliché. He will only offer Himself, His truth, and His undying, unconditional love.

Take some time to consider where you are in the grief process. Write out the names of people who surprised you by walking away. Forgive them. Write out praise to God for those who have remained. And thank Him for being the One who will *never* leave.

_____

_____

_____

_____

_____

_____

_____

_____

_____

# SOMETHING I WILL NEVER SAY

*Ruth Smith*

Normally I do not talk about my experience with losing a baby because it was so long ago and subjects like these were not talked about often. God has put it on my heart (for some unknown reason) to tell you my story because this subject was treated so differently 56 years ago.

My husband and I were married in 1962. We were very much in love and wanted to have a baby as soon as we could. We lived in Louisiana at the time because my husband was in the Army. I still remember the joy we both felt when I became pregnant five months after we were married.

It seemed like a normal pregnancy until the third month, when little things started to happen. At four months, I went to the hospital, and there the nightmare began.

I was taken into a room with two male doctors. All the doctors in those years were male. My husband was not invited into the room. The doctors told me I was having a miscarriage and they needed to "end it." They proceeded to "take the baby out" (the only words they had).

...............................................................................................

They immediately took out the "material" that was in my uterus. There was no mention of the word "baby." I saw them take the contents and throw it in the trash can behind them. I will never forget this picture. It's forever glued to my mind. After cleaning me up, they told me I could go home. We left the hospital in a complete daze, not knowing what had really happened. No one showed us any sympathy in any way.

I realize this is the way things were done at this time, and I do not hold any blame against the doctors. Being an Army hospital, this was the way things worked there.

When we got back to our apartment, my husband called his mother (who was a non-Christian), and she told him she "was so sorry." That was the nicest thing anyone said to us.

My mother and sister (both Christians) said, "don't worry, you will get pregnant again." And they would repeat that phrase over and over. That is something I will never say to someone who has lost a baby.

....................................  ....................................

# DAY 16

As a father has compassion on his children,
so the LORD has compassion
on those who fear him;
for he knows how we are formed,
he remembers that we are dust.
The life of mortals is like grass,
they flourish like a flower of the field;
the wind blows over it and it is gone,
and its place remembers it no more.
But from everlasting to everlasting
the LORD's love is with those who fear Him...

PSALM 103:13–17

Days pass by and the inner places of your heart feel like brittle, weakened pieces of glass. In an instant, anything could cause you to shatter, and a flood of tears and emotions would pour out. Your faith feels flimsy at best. Your questions outnumber your answers, and the truth you know is constantly being threatened with whispered lies from the enemy.

Your Father knows. He sees that you are weak. He hears your questions. . . and it's okay. He knows you are human. You have real doubts, real fears, real wounds, real emotions, a real desire to understand—and He wants to meet you in that. God does not expect us to navigate this life on our own.

I often say, "He's not a 'drop-off' God." He doesn't lead us somewhere and then suddenly hand over the reins, expecting us to suddenly start steering and figuring out the path on our own. This is a journey He wants to take with us; steps He wants to help us with. He knows that within this fallen, broken world there are things we are not equipped to handle or understand.

One of those things is death. God created us for life—ultimately for eternal life. It's hard for us to get our heads and hearts around death, and God knows this. That's why He doesn't expect you to walk this road alone. He sees your broken heart, your wounds, and your confusion. He is here. He loves you. He walks with you, even if you cannot see Him or sense His presence right now.

Speak to Him about your weak places. Write them out, and ask Him to show you where His strength can meet your weakness. Open up His Word and search for how He is strong and mighty to save. Be still and consider the strength that now holds you together, even when you feel like you are falling apart.

_____

_____

_____

_____

_____

_____

_____

_____

_____

He heals the brokenhearted
and binds up their wounds.
He determines the number of the stars
and calls them each by name.
Great is our Lord and mighty in power;
his understanding has no limit.

PSALM 147:3-5

Wounds often leave scars, reminders of a painful moment in life. Moments where we bled, were bruised, and perhaps were broken. Places that, if they were not stitched back together, wouldn't heal properly or completely.

Wounding words, careless actions, ignorant indignation, and sometimes even an absence of understanding can cause wounds. These wounds can intensify injuries that already exist from the losses you already carry.

Your Great Physician and Father sees. He came in the form of a perfect man, Jesus, to save the world. Jesus loves us as we are, where we are. He loves us too much to leave us in these broken places, injured and hurting. He pours over the lacerations a healing balm that only He possesses. He covers the gaping gashes with His own hand, bringing healing you never thought possible.

The scars remain. But He heals the wounds in such a way that the story they leave behind brings an odd joy you can't explain. The story reveals a purpose for the pain endured when the wounds were made. He repairs, He redeems, and He restores.

This God, the maker of all that is, who determines the number of stars in the universe and calls them by name . . . this God, who knows the numbers of hairs on your head and the number of the grains of sand on the beach . . . this all-powerful God, mighty in wisdom and power, still cares about our scrapes and our bruised knees . . . and deeply cares about our crushed and fractured hearts.

Write out the wounds you recognize in yourself today. Perhaps these are wounds that are far beyond the loss of your child. Perhaps these wounds extend from far before the brokenness of loss ravaged your life. Write it out. Cry it out. Talk it out with your Heavenly Physician.

_____

_____

_____

_____

_____

_____

_____

_____

_____

_____

_____

# SUFFER THE LITTLE CHILDREN

*Becki Reiser*

In May of 2000, our seventeen-year-old daughter, Liz, was abducted and murdered. I'm sure you're thinking, "Oh my, what a tragedy," and indeed it was. Some of you are thinking that seventeen is not a baby, or a miscarriage, or stillbirth. You are correct. But you need to know the background to understand how the following story happened.

Our daughter was a strong Christian, closest to the Lord in the months before her death. Yet, on the day the police came to our home, (the day after we found out she had passed away), they had just announced that they had the man in custody and he confessed to the crime. The relief we felt was intense. My husband and I were sitting on the swing on our porch with several other people. It was the only place where we felt we could get air into our lungs. You all know how that feels. For the previous 36 hours, my husband, Jeff, was a rock. He was so strong, and led our family to the understanding that forgiveness was the only way for us to react. We know that God tells us that we must forgive, so that we can be forgiven (Matthew 6:14).

As we sat on that swing, my husband broke down. He sobbed and said, "Oh God, I just need to know where Liz is." I leaned into him and put my arm across him to hold him, as he had done with me previously. Jeff grew quiet, and stopped breathing. In that moment, God gave me a vision. It was as if I was watching a movie. At first, all I could see was our daughter's smiling face. She was looking at something in front of her, but I couldn't see what.

Then, as if a camera was moving out slowly, and I could see more of Liz, then I began to see someone standing behind her. I could see arms opened wide, and he was wearing pure white. No face, only a portion of his body. Then, again the picture widened. I could see Liz laughing, and looking around her. Then I could see the whole picture. Seeing movement as it became clear. There were children in front of her. Many ages, some newborns, infants, toddlers, and even school aged. Many of them were jumping up and down, some were hugging each other, and all were interacting with Liz and the man behind her. Such extraordinary joy I saw. Then I heard the words, "Suffer the little children to come unto me" . . . I knew I was seeing a piece of heaven. Where our daughter was, and where my two miscarried babies were, as well as many other children gone into eternity.

As soon as the words were spoken, Jeff started breathing again. I sat up and shared the vision with him. What amazing HOPE that gave to us!

Reprinted from Becki's book, *Through My Tears: Awash in Forgiveness*. Used by permission.

Those who sow in tears
will reap with songs of joy.
Those who go out weeping,
carrying seed to sow,
will return with songs of joy,
carrying sheaves with them.

PSALM 126:5-6

Have you been sowing tears lately? I believe there have been days that I could have watered acres of our farm fields with them. It seemed impossible that I would ever come out of those weeping fields with a song of joy. How could I possibly have joy through the deepest sorrow of my life?

I recall sowing our child into the ground as I stood over his tiny casket in the frigid January snow. In some strange corner of my mind, I wondered if the blanket I crocheted for him would be warm enough. Another piece of my heart broke off as we walked away, leaving his little body to be planted into the icy clay . . . alone. More than anything, I just wanted to dig him up. I still do.

Every time I drive by the cemetery, I have this bizarre urge to go and dig him out of the ground. He shouldn't be there in the cold, dark soil. My head knows he isn't there. My head knows he lives in the presence of the Almighty. Yet my heart has moments where it hasn't caught up with the knowledge I know to be true. My momma arms long to hold his little body. My momma eyes want to gaze on his little face just one more time. My momma heart wants to hear his noises and giggles. Yet he is sown into the ground in silence. Where is anything remotely resembling joy to be found . . . ever?

Portions of me long to sit in pools of tears for the rest of my existence. Yet there is a difference between godly sorrow and ruminating self-pity. We don't grieve as those who have no hope of ever seeing their babies again. Deep inside, I know that all of our babies are safely in the arms of our Father. These little ones are secure in eternity. This awareness is what gives me the strength to face the days ahead. But this doesn't negate my longing or my pain.

God teaches us that grief and loss are important in this life. Instead of pat answers, He wants us to go through the grief process and glean a harvest. It's tempting to rush grief, gloss over it, ignore it even, but if we allow it to do its work, an abundant harvest awaits us. Our weeping must not deter our sowing. We must set our minds and hearts, determined to gather good things from our times of affliction.

Spend time in prayer. Ask God to show you what good thing He is sowing into you during this time of affliction. Remember the good things He has brought you through moments of difficulty in the past. Write down the harvest from previous afflictions. Write out your hope for good things to come from this grueling road. For example, I see that my heart is forever changed toward others who experience loss. He has given me compassion that I did not possess before. I have been drawn into deeper knowledge of His character and presence that brings joy and goodness out of affliction.

_____

_____

_____

Then they cried out to the LORD in their trouble,
and he brought them out of their distress.
He stilled the storm to a whisper;
the waves of the sea were hushed.
They were glad when it grew calm,
and He guided them to their desired haven.
Let them give thanks to the LORD his unfailing love
and his wonderful deeds for mankind.

PSALM 107:28–31

It seems a lifetime ago that things felt even remotely normal to me, whatever "normal" is.

Sailors at sea often witness rescue from life-threatening peril. They also witness the beauty of the waters, sunrises, and sunsets. They behold waters both calm as glass and tempestuously dangerous. Were it not for the storms and the tossing of their ships, they could not appreciate the calm. Were it not for crying out in the middle of impossible storms, they would not witness the power and strength of God to bring them through alive.

In the storm of loss, it seems as though a piece of us has died, but something new is being birthed in us. It is new life found in complete dependence on God: survival for the next moment, the next day, and the next breath. This dependence draws us near. We find ourselves grateful for days when peace surpasses our understanding and we sense that our wounds ache a little less. We see His unfailing love and mercy meet us in the middle of the storm and hold us as raging waters pass over.

We know His presence is with us as the winds threaten to throw us off course. We dig our roots deeper into His truth and cling tightly. Our hearts are broken, and they cannot be trusted to clearly see where our feet need to land on this path. So with what we know, we hold fast to the anchor of our souls. We remain grateful for His love. As we cry out, He brings us the peace of His presence. We are glad as we rest in the calm of His hand.

Write out a prayer of gratitude. There is always something to be grateful for.

_____

_____

_____

_____

_____

_____

_____

_____

_____

_____

_____

_____

# APRIL LYNN

*Loren Essenburg*

$M$ay 2, 1979, was a date that had a major impact in history. *My* history. I was a young man of nineteen preparing for life as a newlywed and soon-to-be first-time father. We had the baby's room ready and decorated. Crib, check. Diaper bag, check. Bottles and formula, check. And because we didn't know the gender of the baby, we had clothes for either a girl or a boy. Everything was in order!

My wife got pregnant before we were married, so I "manned up" and asked her to marry me. Fortunately, she said *yes*! The wedding was in January of 1979, approximately four months before the baby was due. We began our lives together as husband and wife. A new world awaited us!

The pregnancy went well until the actual due date. We had an appointment for a checkup. The doctor noted the child's heartbeat was soft, but he didn't seem concerned.

We only had one car at that time, so my wife drove me to work in case she went into labor. We got more excited each day. Our baby would be with us soon.

One day I got a call from the security guard that my wife had gone into labor and she was going to pick me up on the way to the hospital. She'd already contacted the doctor and let him know.

Our excitement grew as we went into the delivery room. My wife had a normal delivery with no issues. They took our

..................................................................................

little baby girl, April Lynn, out of the room as soon as she was born. Then the doctor came back and quickly explained our baby was having problems they needed to check out.

Time just seemed to *stop*.

The nurses moved us to a post-delivery room. We waited there for the doctor to come back with our baby. But he returned without her. He quietly said, "I'm so sorry. Your daughter didn't make it."

I didn't know what to do or what to say, so I held my wife and we cried. The doctor said they had to finish cleaning up my wife, so I was asked to leave. I didn't want to leave her.

I went to the waiting room and fell on my knees and cried some more. I pounded the cement floor with my bare fists repeating, "Why me? Why us?!" Our world was gone, destroyed. Our child would never say our names. Our child was never coming home.

Forty years have passed. There are very few days I don't think about our daughter. But the nightmares are gone. It was His grace and mercy that healed the wounds. I realize now that April is home. She is in heaven with the greatest Father ever! I thank God for bringing me through this and knowing I will see her again!

.............................              .....................................

# DAY 20

So we don't look at the troubles we can see now; rather, we fix our gaze on things that cannot be seen. For the things we see now will soon be gone, but the things we cannot see will last forever.

2 Corinthians 4:18 NLT

I sat staring at the casket. I put on a brave face as I silently mourned. Embarrassed and fighting guilt, I realized my thoughts were not fixed on mourning the death of my dear father-in-law. Rather, they were focused on the loss of our fifth child in my first trimester, as my body had betrayed me yet again. My invisible grief made me feel like I was going to implode.

I gazed at the casket, the American flag draped over the cover and crowned with a cascade of flowers. I listened to blurred words of hope—words meant to honor my sweet father-in-law after his courageous battle with cancer. Yet somehow, as I sat quietly in physical and emotional pain, I felt as though the words were also for my sweet baby.

Your view on life shifts after walking a road like this. Questions hang in the sky like a fog. We can fear to ask our questions aloud, especially when they include questioning God, His goodness, or His plans. It is through lament that we draw closer to Him in honesty. He meets us in our lament. He brings us truth, comfort, and eternal hope through relationship with Him.

For it is through Him that we will be reunited with our children again. As we focus on our hope and life eternal, we fear death a little less. We realize that part of us already resides in heaven, and we will one day be joined with that tiny life again.

What do you hope for? Do you have hope in Jesus? Where are you today? Where has the road of grief taken you this week?

_____

_____

_____

_____

_____

_____

_____

_____

_____

_____

_____

_____

_____

_____

## DAY 21

Praise the LORD, my soul;
all my inmost being, praise his holy name.
Praise the LORD, my soul, and forget not His benefits—
who forgives all your sins and heals all your diseases,
who redeems your life from the pit
and crowns you with love and compassion,
who satisfies your desires with good things
so that your youth is renewed like the eagle's.

PSALM 103:1-5

I don't know about you, but on this journey I've had to do a lot of preaching to myself. On those mornings that seem impossible to face, I have to instruct myself how to respond when I hear someone else is pregnant and force the obligatory smile to gush over someone else's newborn.

Those days make me weary. How about you? I have to remind myself, just like the psalmist, "Praise the Lord . . . even in the depths of heartache. Praise the Lord . . . even when you can barely lift your head, open your eyes, or stop the tears. Praise the Lord . . . in the middle of the baby dedication as you watch others stand where your feet should be. Praise the Lord . . . with whatever you have left in this moment. Praise the Lord."

Incredible things happen when we offer honest praise: disease healed, physical and emotional wounds healed, places redeemed that we thought were completely lost, and, best of all, the beautiful gifts of forgiveness and freedom! We can stand in gratitude for these things and more, even in the middle of horrific loss. When we choose to praise in the pain, we gain a purer awareness of His goodness and mercy pursuing us all the days of our lives.

Write out a gratitude list. It can be for anything, even chocolate! Refer back to your bunches of blessings on those days when it's hard to see the sun. Give thanks.

_____

_____

_____

_____

_____

_____

_____

_____

_____

_____

_____

_____

_____

# SOMETHING BEAUTIFUL

## *Dana Symons*

"I'm not seeing a gestational sac."

The words from my ultrasound tech at my six-week appointment echoed through my mind like a bad dream, resounding off the emptiness I felt inside—as empty as my womb.

There was no pregnancy. I was pregnant. And then, I wasn't.

Blood tests confirmed an early missed miscarriage. This came after seven years of infertility and a horrible experience going through IVF with endometriosis—a painful process that garnered us just a single embryo, our last chance at having biological kids.

My heart was heavy with sorrow. This was the loss of not only our child but also a dream. I had finally let myself get excited and believe that I was going to be a mom, and now my child was gone and the role of mother was swept away from me. Where would we go from here? How would we pick up the pieces of a broken dream?

Grief is real. And it is hard. And that's okay. It's okay to not be okay for a while. As I process my grief over time, peace and healing will come. Through my tears, I am beginning to realize that I've misplaced something somewhere in this process. Hope.

Hope, when misplaced, is a fragile thing. Easily broken. Quickly dashed. And hope that is crushed is toxic to the soul.

> Why, my soul, are you downcast?
> Why so disturbed within me?
> Put your hope in God,
> for I will yet praise him,
> my Savior and my God.
>
> PSALM 42:5

..................................................................................

When I put my hope in my own plans, I'm at risk for disappointment. But when I put my hope in God's plans, I'm reminded that this is not the end of our story. It is only the end of a chapter. God can redeem even the worst and most broken things in our lives to bring forth something beautiful.

While the sorrow will linger, perhaps forever, life is not without joy and gratitude. I am so thankful for my husband and our relationship. I'm grateful for our home, our jobs, and our dog. And I'm so thankful for all the loving and supportive friends and family we have, many of whom have walked this journey with us. I am thankful for the chance to try IVF, for the knowledge that we exhausted all of our options, and for the opportunity to experience the joy of pregnancy, even if just for a moment in time. And so this tiny life, though not destined for this world, will be forever in our hearts and perhaps be a catalyst for changes yet to come.

It has only been about a week since we discovered our loss at the time of this writing, so what happens from here is not yet clear. But we still have the desire to share our home and our love with children and to pour life into others. And I believe God will honor those desires, perhaps in ways we have not yet imagined.

..........................................                    ..........................................

The LORD is my strength and my defense;
he has become my salvation.

PSALM 118:14

The darker the cave, the closer to the light I need to be. It's difficult to find anything in the dark. Unless the path is well lit, it can be impossible to see where we are, where we are going, or what danger may lurk ahead. Unless I have a flashlight or torch as I step into the darkness, it's impossible to find a light source once I'm immersed in the blackness.

I wrestle with the question of God's goodness to me. After all, if God is ultimately good and loves me like He claims, why would He allow such horrific things to happen in my life? Why would He want to watch me suffer as I hold my dead baby? Why would He allow people to get pregnant and have children who don't want them, will abuse them, or will get rid of them? Does He not see the longing of my heart? Does He not care about my pain? I toss about in my beliefs. My faith falters as I begin asking Him these questions aloud.

If I don't have a proper theology of suffering, I destroy the truth I know about God's character.

When I forget that I live in a fallen world, I blame God. I blame God for the failings of the fallen. I am slow to call to mind the multitudes of ways He has shown His merciful goodness even in the midst of pain, sorrow, and loss. The deep knowledge of His character, His kindness, His goodness, His steadfast love . . . these things must be established prior to the dark, cave-like moments.

We choose what we believe. Many times, we choose our feelings as well. If we remain close to the ultimate source of light, it will undoubtedly help us to walk through this dark cave of loss and sorrow in the days to come.

What do you believe about the goodness of God? How can you draw nearer to your light source? List some character attributes you know to be true, even if you struggle to feel them right now.

_____

_____

_____

_____

_____

_____

_____

_____

_____

_____

_____

_____

_____

You turned my wailing into dancing;
you removed my sackcloth and clothed me with joy,
that my heart may sing your praises and not be silent.
LORD my God, I will praise you forever.

PSALM 30:11-12

As we walk forward without our precious little ones, joy is often covered by the darkened clouds of sorrow. We grieve the secondary losses that come as we remember them on their birthdays, holidays, and the empty place at the dinner table. As we lean into lament and draw closer to the Savior, we see that there is One who is sovereign. We remember that He has already been victorious over sin and death. The battle is won; the victory has already been claimed!

We know without doubt that our child is in heaven with our loving Father, held, healed, and whole. For this truth and His victory—our victory—we can be thankful. We can dance in the rain and sing through our sorrow. In the middle of pain, we can give thanks. We can have hope. We can even have joy, all because we have Jesus.

We know that we cry out to a God who has the power to change circumstances, but more importantly, this God can change our perspective in those circumstances. We can rest knowing our child is safe and whole in the loving arms of the Almighty, and one day we will be there too . . . together.

We walk forward, fully human, but with an eternal per-spective. Filled with thanksgiving and hope, our tears of mourning shift to tears of joy for a God who cares about even the tiniest details and most mundane moments of our lives. He is with us, for us, and never leaves us—walking with us through the shadows of death, restoring us, and filling us with joy.

Heavenly Father,

There are days when joy seems the furthest thing from my heart. Thank You for being a God that will allow me to be honest, pouring out my anger, my questions, and my sorrows. I know that You use everything we hand over to You. Oh, Lord, I hand over this pain, this grief, this sorrow . . . I hand it over to You and ask that You redeem it somehow, Lord. Somehow, give me eyes to see Your mighty hand using this trial for something good and eternal.

In Jesus' Name, amen.

Write your own prayer of thanksgiving as you consider your valley.

_____

_____

_____

_____

_____

_____

_____

_____

# A FAMILY OF SIX

*Anna Read*

I knew.

I realized it with a thrill of shock and fear on the very first day: I was pregnant with our fourth baby. But my cluttered mind was not ready for another year of mood swings and sleeplessness and dirty diapers. Our youngest was 8 months old. My body had barely recovered from the last pregnancy. My husband was stressed out already. Our house only had four bedrooms. We were planning to travel the week I was due. There was no space for this baby—not in our house, not on our calendar, not in my heart.

The days ticked by, dragging with them the extra exhaustion of pregnancy.

And then one day, I felt my first glimmer of joy over our new family member. Still, there were times I felt an avalanche of fear, uncertainty, and anxiety.

But God knew what He was doing: when I let Him in, He gave me peace in slivers. One day, it was strengthened by my husband's first smile over the baby. The next, it was deepened by my daughters' excitement over bunk beds. Then came the fun of fitting the perfect name to the life growing inside me. I didn't have answers to everything. I knew it would be hard. But I could believe that it would all be worth it.

And then I started bleeding. Lots of explanations for that, the doctor's office assured me over the phone. Friends said it had happened to them. Through needles, tense appointments, and desperate prayers, I made excuses for the lack of a heartbeat. We waited for test results. The phone call came while I was cuddling my youngest. Before the cold twist of shock worked all the way through me, before the loss felt real, God gave me gratitude. Gratitude for the one I held, gratitude that I was not alone, and gratitude that this was not the end for my baby and me.

Yes, the end came before most of my baby's beginnings. We were left with no funeral, no coffin, no grave, no pictures, no memories. No medical bills, no pain, no social security number. But we were not left with nothing. We had the God who made us all, who knew all our days, even if they ended before birth, and of course we had heaven.

I spent the months following the miscarriage living out my emotions through writing a sad fictional story about two people who don't get the chance they deserve to love each other this side of eternity. We named our baby Augustine, and I added the appropriate birthstone to my necklace of all my kids' birth months.

And then as we sang hymns together at Christmas, I felt God remind me that somewhere—even louder and more joyful than our church's family Christmas service—Augustine was worshipping, too.

We were, and always will be, a family of six.

## DAY 24

Whatever is true, whatever is noble,
whatever is right, whatever is pure,
whatever is lovely, whatever is admirable—
if anything is excellent or praiseworthy—
think about such things.

PHILIPPIANS 4:8

I don't know about you, but some days it's really difficult to jump off of the "rehearse my pain" merry-go-round. I cycle through the trauma, the images, the sounds, the smells, the emotion of the loss, and I plummet into darkness, anxiety, and deep sorrow. If I ruminate there too long, I end up depressed to a point that I find it difficult to get out of bed. I've learned to set a limit on those thoughts.

But I *do* need to process them. Yes, I should not gloss them over or pretend I'm in a better place than I am.

We should never gloss over grief. Grief is not a process one can rush. It is also not something that can be ignored or avoided. It is journey with many stages, all of which have been created by God to help us cope and heal. This healing is not linear. One Christian therapist described it as more like being on a spiral staircase where the healing stages are revisited time and time again, but from different perspectives.

As we move through our grief process, honestly sharing our feelings with God, we begin to be able to breathe again, see beauty again. We begin to find that we have grown, forged by fire into a new creation. We are able once again to think on those truths and things that are right, noble, pure, lovely, and admirable in this present day. We can offer praise and rejoice in the fact that our sovereign God is with us, ever present and unchanging regardless of our pain.

Make a list of things that are true, noble, right, pure, lovely, admirable, excellent, and praiseworthy.

_____

_____

_____

_____

_____

_____

_____

_____

_____

_____

_____

_____

# DAY 25

I love the LORD, for he heard my voice;
he heard my cry for mercy,
Because He turned his ear to me,
I will call on Him as long as I live.
The cords of death entangled me,
the anguish of the grave came upon me;
I was overcome by trouble and sorrow.
Then I called on the name of the LORD;
"LORD, save me!"

PSALM 116:1-4

Often when crying out for mercy, we miss the mercy we've already been given. We forget the places where God has gifted us with His merciful presence. We overlook the spaces He has mercifully occupied with His love. We cry out for release from the chains of the pain in which we find ourselves entrapped. We feel overcome by death, nearly choked by its noose. Nothing can prepare us for staring into the face of our dead child, hearing the words "This one isn't going to make it," or seeing another negative pregnancy test. Nothing can prime us for the overflow of suffocating anguish that death brings.

However, it is when we remember His faithfulness in times past that we can be encouraged to know that He will be faithful in this journey, too. He is with us, and because of the death of Jesus on the cross, He now holds the victory over sin and death. He made a way for healing. He made a way for life to come through death (John 3:16).

Mercy means we walked away. We broke relationship with Him as we chose to become our own gods and chose to be above God. God chose to mend that relationship by offering a mercy we could never find anywhere else. God chose to heal what was broken and offer Himself. This doesn't free us from consequences, but it does give us hope.

How are you doing these days at focusing on God's faithfulness in times past? How are you doing standing on the truth that His faithfulness does not run out and His presence does not leave us? Write out where you are in a prayer to Him. Remember, it's so very important that you do this from the depths of honesty in your heart. Cry out to Him; He hears and sees.

_____

_____

_____

_____

_____

_____

_____

_____

_____

_____

_____

_____

# GRIEVING WITH HOPE: OLIVER'S STORY

*Emily Smith*

It was my husband's birthday, and we were at the park for a picnic with our eighteen-month-old son. Tucked in the picnic basket was a card with a stick figure drawing of our family, an arrow pointing to my pregnant belly, and a caption that read, "Surprise, we're pregnant!" We were hoping for another baby, and this was the perfect birthday gift for the man who loves being a dad.

Three months later, I was sitting in the midwife's office for my 16-week checkup. I came alone because the pregnancy had been picture-perfect so far—I had even started feeling the baby move a couple of weeks previously. Now the midwife was struggling to find the heartbeat with the Doppler monitor, so we headed for the ultrasound room.

As soon as the picture came up, we knew, yet all of us wanted it to be untrue. The midwife, the nurse, and I stared at the monitor, willing my baby to move, willing his heart to beat. But there was only stillness and silence, confirming our fear that my baby was gone. No warning, no visible reason—just suddenly and very unexpectedly gone. Late miscarriages (between 14 and 20 weeks) are rare, happening in around only two percent of pregnancies, and in most cases, the cause is unknown.

Like so many others who walk this road, we were utterly heartbroken. Shocked. Confused. Sad. Weary. It was the week of Thanksgiving, yet instead of relaxing and enjoying the holiday, we prepared for a labor and delivery happening much too early for a child we would not take home. We made decisions on how to honor and celebrate our baby, what to call him, and what to do with his tiny little body.

Miscarriage is a stark reminder that the world is broken and fragile. The world may look solid and trustworthy, but the reality is that Christ is our only solid ground. Jesus is good and trustworthy, even when the days are hard. His promises are true, and He remains solid even when our world is shaking.

In the midst of our grief, my husband and I found hope in Psalm 139:15-16 (ESV, emphasis added): "My frame was not hidden from you, when I was being made in secret, intricately woven in the depths of the earth. Your eyes saw my unformed substance; *in your book were written, every one of them, the days that were formed for me, when as yet there was none of them.*"

The length of my life, your life, and our babies' lives were determined before time began. That truth gives us assurance that my baby and your baby were not accidents. God ordains every day of life, and nothing can change that. At the end of that week, our son Oliver was stillborn, 7 inches and 3.5 ounces of perfection. His life was not an accident, and his death was not a surprise to God. Although we miss him, we are thankful that this life is not the end and that we will spend eternity with him.

# DAY 26

[Speak] to one another with psalms, hymns,
and songs from the Spirit. Sing and make
music in your heart to the Lord, always giving
thanks to God the Father for everything,
in the name of our Lord Jesus Christ.

EPHESIANS 5:19-20

We may not always be able to give thanks to God in our difficulties. I know in the middle of my losses, praising, singing, and making (or, in my case, writing) music was next to impossible. I could barely read more than several sentences, let alone sing three words. So I chose to make music in my heart—music in the groaning. Singing through the sorrow.

It was in those moments that I found the most important thing in the world to me. It was then, when all else I longed for was stripped away, that I saw Jesus. The question was not how much of Him I had, but how much of me did He have?

I couldn't thank Him for allowing my babies to be taken from me. I couldn't thank Him or be glad about the circumstances of my suffering, but I found I could praise Him and thank Him for what He was building in me. I could worship Him for the beautiful aspects of His character that He was revealing to me through this path. I could give thanks to Him for being present to share in my sorrow with His peace and understanding.

How much of you does He have? How is He revealing more of Himself to you on in these days?

Thank Him.

_____

_____

_____

_____

_____

_____

_____

_____

_____

_____

_____

_____

_____

_____

_____

The LORD will vindicate me;
your love, LORD, endures forever—
do not abandon the works of your hands.

PSALM 138:8

You are God's deeply loved creation. He loves you beyond comprehension and is orchestrating a beautiful symphony, a melody that can only be sung to the world through your life. From the moment He began to fashion you, He had a purpose and plan spinning in place, a way for you to touch the world in ways no other soul can.

I often consider how the lives of my babies have changed me. Even though their tiny feet never walked this earth, they have impacted my life and made a difference in the lives of others. What more could my mother heart long for?

Dear friend, our stories are not done being written. We do not know what joy or pain tomorrow may bring. We *do* know that God is writing and creating something beyond what we can imagine or hope for. We can depend on Him to finish what He has begun. As we lay our lives before Him, relinquishing control, we know that He will not leave us. As we abide in Him, He will hold us close. As we walk forward, He will walk with us. He will remain faithful to the purpose He intended for us and see us through.

This song in a minor key is part of a greater work that He will use to bring hope and encouragement to the world.

Even though it's hard now, we give thanks for the story He is writing. Even though we do not see the ending, we trust and give thanks. We give thanks that He set a plan and purpose in motion before we drew a breath and that He will see it to completion, no matter what comes.

_____

_____

_____

_____

_____

_____

_____

_____

_____

_____

_____

_____

_____

_____

# THE SECRET THINGS

*Rebekah Mitchell*

On June 24, 1995, my baby, Jonathan Daniel Mitchell, was stillborn. He was delivered weighing 2 pounds and 12 ounces and with the umbilical cord wrapped around his head, body, and left leg.

His stillbirth rocked me to the core physically, emotionally, and mainly spiritually. I thought God and I had a plan. I believed without wavering that our baby would be a testament of the Lord's faithfulness. The doctors predicted an early delivery, and I firmly believed if they were correct, then Jonathan would beat all the odds of complications that come with a premature birth. Never in a million years did I dream he would die!

The weeks and months following Jonathan's stillbirth were the worst days of my life. After months of doubting and questioning everything I had ever believed about the Lord, I finally experienced spiritual healing. I accepted that God's ways are higher than our ways, and He knows every one of our days before any of them come to be, including my little

Jonathan's. God knew from the beginning that my little son would never breathe a breath outside my womb and that the secret things belong to Him.

After this spiritual epiphany, I asked God what plan He had for me with this loss. Over the next several weeks, He impressed upon me to start a ministry for families who have suffered the death of a baby; thus the birth of MEND (Mommies Enduring Neonatal Death). We are a Christian nonprofit organization that reaches out to families who have suffered the death of a baby through miscarriage, stillbirth, or early infant death. To learn how MEND can support you, visit our website at mend.org and let us comfort you with the comfort we ourselves have received from God.

Rebekah Mitchell
Founder and President, Mommies Enduring Neonatal Death
mend.org

I heard a loud shout from the throne, saying, "Look,
God's home is now among his people! He will live with
them, and they will be his people. God himself will be
with them. He will wipe every tear from their eyes,
and there will be no more death or sorrow or crying
or pain. All these things are gone forever."

REVELATION 21:3–4 (NLT)

Grief without hope is a dark place. As followers of Jesus, we
don't need to wander in darkness. Though we may feel like we
are stuck in a blackened room as we grieve, the truth is that
we have been gifted the greatest light of all. We need only to
plug in to the power source to turn it on.

We may not feel hope, joy, or even the slightest ounce of
happiness, but we can journey forward with our loss knowing
that Jesus gave us courage to do so through the mighty power
of the cross. We travel forward, clinging to the promise that
He will be faithful to the end. We hold tightly to the vision of
the day when we will unite in wholeness and holiness with
Him and those we have loved while on this earth. This truth,
my friends, is praiseworthy.

As we choose clear thinking about the end of our days, as
we hold tight to the truth of His word and promises, it helps us
to see clearly in our present pain.

What do you think it will be like to be united with Him?
Imagine the day you will see the faces of those you've said

goodbye to. Write about your heart in that moment. Give thanks to God for His faithful promises of what is coming!

_____

_____

_____

_____

_____

_____

_____

_____

_____

_____

_____

_____

_____

_____

_____

_____

## DAY 29

Praise be to the God and Father of our Lord Jesus
Christ, the Father of compassion and the God of
all comfort, who comforts us in all our troubles,
so that we can comfort those in any trouble with
the comfort we ourselves receive from God. For just
as we share abundantly in the sufferings of Christ,
so also our comfort abounds through Christ.

2 CORINTHIANS 1:3–5

As I consider the paths I've walked along this journey, I realize the circumstances of my story are not unique. Countless others have endured the same hardships and worse. We cannot compare the roads we have traveled. Your grief is your grief. Mine is mine.

Since I was a small child, I longed for the events in my life to have meaning. If there was a tragedy, I wanted to know the reason. I began looking for ways that God could use any heartbreak in my life for something . . . *anything* . . . good.

Sometimes there were nights darker than I could hardly stand, and I doubted that any good could come from them. I sat still in the quiet yearning for some semblance of meaning in the trial. I longed for God to use the pain for a purpose. I wanted Him to use me to comfort others; to walk with them and love them like He loves me.

God began giving me glimpses of my calling early in my life. I knew that I was created to tell people that Jesus loves them. I knew that I was His and that He had a plan for me. I had no idea what it was early on, and in a million years I never would have guessed that this is the path He would have chosen for me. However, we often find that our purpose is birthed in pain and our calling is found in our crisis.

Through it all, our faithful God is forever planting seeds for deeper faith and deeper relationship, and an opportunity to live out everything we were created for.

_____

_____

_____

_____

_____

_____

_____

_____

_____

_____

_____

_____

_____

_____

# SHADOWS

## *Melinda Ganka*

I would be thirty-one weeks pregnant now, but our fourth baby was delivered into the arms of Jesus on January 9, when I was thirteen weeks along. I am sharing this not only to support other moms who have quietly endured miscarriages, but also because something inside me needs to break the silence.

While I am truly at peace with the loss of my baby, standing firmly in the knowledge she is perfect and whole in the company of my King, my heart still aches when I think about . . . me. I hate doing two things: discouraging people and focusing on me, yet here I am talking about my loss.

The beauty of pregnancy is that it is obvious. Beautiful visual cues allow everyone to see and know that joy and beauty are growing inside you—a blessed gift from God. For me, the pain of miscarriage is the silence.

Picking up my son from preschool recently, I found myself in conversation with a teacher and another mom discussing the mom's estimated due date in August. For the first time in my life, I looked away from a pregnant woman. This new pain hurt too much—standing in the echo of congratulations and well wishes and thinking, "That would be me too."

The pain was unexpected. During the first few weeks following our loss, I was blessed—completely washed in comfort and peace (Philippians 4:4-7). How amazing is our Father, who

....................................................................

created everything yet knows our pain and still holds us in His great compassionate hands (Deuteronomy 31:6) (1 Peter 5:7)!

The salt on the wounds of miscarriage are shadows—shadows of what I would look like, how many weeks along I would be, the preparations that won't take place.

Shadows no one sees but me.

Silence, in which the joys, excitement, and congratulations echo, not for me, but for other blessed women.

This journey has enlightened me to a side of motherhood I never could have understood or related to before my loss (2 Corinthians 1:3-4). To my dear friends who have endured miscarriages, infertility, and infant death, I want to say I love you so much and pray for your comfort when salt stings your wounds.

I am filled with joy that our baby is exactly where God called her to be. Still, I await her estimated due date. Perhaps getting through this "would-have-been" time will lessen the shadows and quiet the echoes. No matter what lies on the other side of my due date, I walk this journey with my God and King.

Never alone, always heard, forever loved.

Shout for joy to the LORD, all the earth.
Worship the LORD with gladness;
come before Him with joyful songs.
Know that the LORD is God,
It is he who made us, and we are his;
we are his people, the sheep of his pasture.
Enter his gates with thanksgiving
and his courts with praise;
give thanks to him and praise his name.
For the LORD is good
and his love endures forever;
his faithfulness continues through
all generations.

PSALM 100

From ashes new life rises. Death births new life. This is only accomplished through God. No one and nothing but the Almighty brings something new through death, for no one else is God but He. He is worthy of praise, even through our tears. Our Creator, the one who gives us all things—life, breath and purpose—is worthy of our praise regardless of the pain of the moment.

We must often choose to praise as an act of will. Sometimes the best we can do is to choose to point our minds and feet in the direction of the Creator God. We choose to believe that He is with us. We choose to praise Him for who He is and not live dependent on good circumstances for that truth.

Worship is a healing balm for grief. When we honestly worship with our deepest soul, even broken worship becomes a great gift to the Almighty—and to us as well. For though we can find ourselves questioning His goodness in these moments, through worship we are ultimately reminded of His steadfast love for us. And as we humble ourselves and honestly cry out, we remind our hearts of His faithfulness in the past.

He treasures the offerings we bring, whether in the middle of darkness or delight. We can trust His goodness in our present and our future. This is true even and *especially* when we can't see an end to our suffering.

He has never left us and He never will.

_____

_____

_____

_____

_____

_____

_____

_____

_____

_____

_____

_____

# HEAVEN'S PLAYGROUND

Sometimes I imagine
a sea of shining faces
Warm sunshine and blue skies
and children running free
And suddenly I'm smiling
to see you there with Jesus
to know you're home and happy
means everything to me

That'll you'll never know pain
You'll only know love
You'll never know tears
in the land of joy above
Where laughter is the only sound
on Heaven's playground

Sometimes when I miss you
sorrow casts a shadow
I linger with the sadness
and feel the things I feel
But then I remember
in this very moment
You're living in His presence
Forever you are healed

and...

You'll never know pain
You'll only know love
You'll never know tears
in the land of joy above
Where laughter is the only sound
on Heaven's playground

The only way these arms could let you go
is to know whose arms would take you in
The one who loved you first will hold you
until I hold you again

You'll never know pain
You'll only know love
You'll never know tears
in the land of joy above
Where laughter is the only sound
Where laughter is the only sound
on Heaven's playground

## SONG CREDITS

......................................................................................

### *Before We Said Hello*
*Sung by Becky Nordquist*

Produced by Kent Hooper and Steve Siler for Music for the Soul

Orchestra arranged and conducted by Phillip Keveren
and recorded at Oceanway, Nashville, TN

Piano: Phillip Keveren

Guitar: Mark Baldwin

Violin: David Davidson (leader), David Angell (contractor),
Conni Ellisor, MaryKathryn VanOsdale, Janet Darnall,
WeiTsun Chang, Carrie Bailey, Jenny Bifano, Erin
Hall, Ali Hoffman, Alicia Enstrom, Katelyn Kelly,
Zeneba Bowers, Stefan Petrescu

Viola: Simona Rusu, Betsy Lamb, Seanad Chang, Chris Farrell

Cello: Anthony LaMarchina, Sari Reist, Julia Tanner, Kevin Bate

Bass: Jack Jezzro, Quentin Flowers

Flute: Erik Gratton

Clarinet: Emily Bowland

Oboe: Grace Woodworth

French Horn: Jennifer Kummer, Beth Beeson

Background vocals: Dan Mitchell

Vocals recorded at The House of Big, Franklin, TN

Mixed by Kent Hooper

### *Heaven's Playground*

*Sung by Becky Nordquist*

Produced by Kent Hooper and Steve Siler for Music for the Soul

Rhythm section recorded by Randy Poole at The Poole Room,
Franklin, TN

Assistant engineer: Greg McGinnis

Piano: Chris Phillips

Guitar: Mike Payne

Bass: Matt Pierson

Drums: Scott Williamson

The Sacred Arts string and woodwind ensemble arranged and
conducted by Phillip Keveren and recorded at The House of Big,
Franklin, TN

Background vocals: Shelly Justice, Debi Selby, and Terry White

Vocals recorded at The House of Big, Franklin, TN

Mixed by Kent Hooper

To download *Before We Said Hello* and *Heaven's Playground* free use the
QR code provided or visit musicforthesoul.org/resources/bwsh-hp

# ACKNOWLEDGMENTS

...................................................................................

*Becky Nordquist would like to thank:*

Steve Siler and Music for the Soul for creating a project that will encourage healing and hope for those who walk through life with this sorrow. Steve, you are dear to me. I'm grateful for God crossing our paths and how he is using you to bring further healing to my heart.

My precious David . . . my love, my leader, my brother in Christ. I could never have gotten through this without you praying over me and walking with me. Our story—God's glory.

My babies—thank you for hugs and happy laughs in the middle of the dark places . . . you are my joy bombs.

My dear family and friends . . . for walking with me. Staying present in the middle of difficulty. Your prayers and encouragement have carried us.

Our many supporters, both financial and prayer warriors.

The Speak Up conference and Carol Kent, Monica Schmelter—media consulting, John Chisum & NCS.

Above all—my Jesus . . . without whom I could not breathe or withstand this life.

*Steve Siler would like to thank:*

Shelly Beach for editorial guidance, Tim Beals and the talented team at Credo House Publishers for their work and expertise, Corey Niemchick and the gang at Storytelling Pictures, Linda and Bob Blair for jump-starting the project, and Lynn McCain for asking, "Where is the book?"

The leadership team at Music for the Soul: Suzanne Foster, John Cozart, Shelly Beach, Susan Brantley, Dawn Damon, and Judi Reid.

All of our faithful prayer partners and financial supporters—we couldn't do it without you.

Our music creation team: co-producer Kent Hooper, arranger Phillip Keveren, co-writer Tony Wood, and all the amazing musicians and engineers who brought their A-game.

Those of you who shared your stories with us along the way—you are a constant source of inspiration!

My wife, Meredith, for editing "the minister of verbosity."

Becky—you share the love of Jesus with everyone you touch. The light pours out of you. You are the heart and soul of this project.

And of course, the Lord Jesus Christ for being the compassionate healer.

# A NOTE
# FROM THE AUTHOR

.....................................................................................

$M$y friend, several years ago in my quiet time with the Lord, I asked, "What can I do to bring You the greatest glory while I'm still here on earth?"

He told me to "Walk in the freedom I paid so dearly for."

I said, "Yes, Lord."

Part of my journey has included saying "Yes" to walking through whatever doors He placed in front of me. This project is the result of relinquishing my "right" to understand why things have happened in my life and, instead, to fix my eyes on the "Who" behind every "Why?"

About me?

I am a Jesus follower. I'm an artist type married to a logically-minded engineer. Dave and I live on a hobby farm in West Michigan, complete with chickens, horses, dogs, every stray cat in the county (it seems), and April the goat. We have eight children here on earth (blended family) and six children in heaven.

Dave and I went through a two-year hurricane of loss. We endured the loss of five pregnancies and the stillbirth of our son, Niklas. During that time we also lost my mom, my father-in-law, my brother, extended family members, and friends. I even lost my dear friend Lisa, who herself had experienced infant loss and was so helpful to me after Niklas' passing.

But nothing tore through my soul like my miscarriages and placing our Niklas in the frozen earth.

In spite of life's deepest sorrows, I know what it means to walk in freedom. I love sharing the word of God through speaking, singing, leading worship, blogging, writing, and recording music.

Whatever we lay down before the Father, He picks up and redeems and restores in ways we never dreamed possible.

Ephesians 3:20-21
Proverbs 3:5-6

Made in United States
North Haven, CT
19 February 2022

16288754R00057